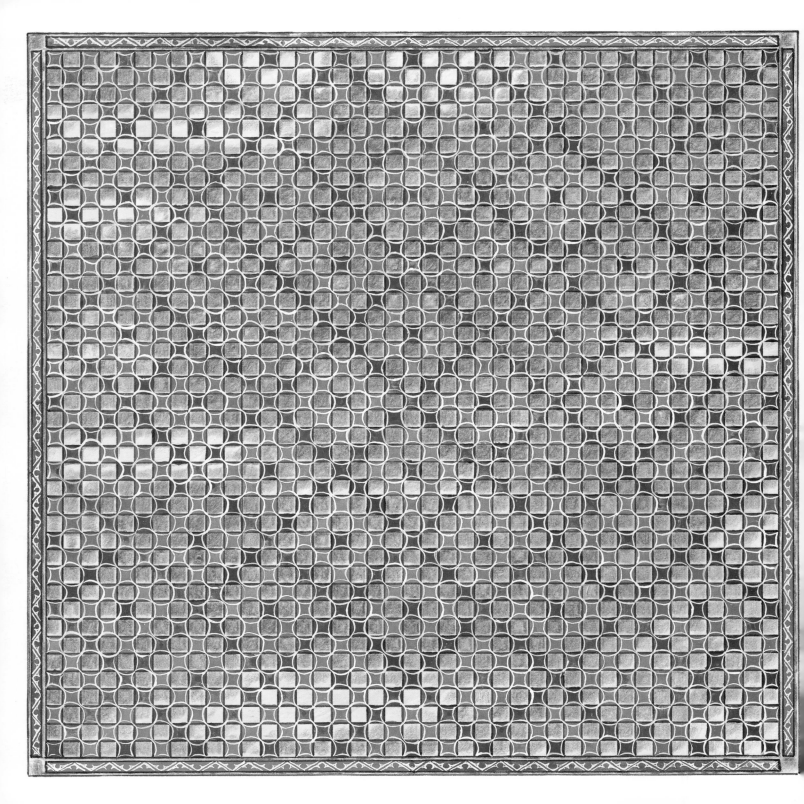

For Pandora   S.H.
For my parents   J.W.

Text copyright © 1985 by Selina Hastings
Illustrations copyright © 1985 by Juan Wijngaard

First published in Great Britain in 1985 by
Walker Books Ltd.

Printed in Hong Kong by South China Printing Company

First Mulberry Edition, 1987
4 5 6 7 8 9 10

Library of Congress Cataloging in Publication Data
Hastings, Selina.
    Sir Gawain and the loathly lady.
    Summary: After a horrible hag saves King Arthur's
life by answering a riddle, Sir Gawain agrees to marry
her and thus releases her from an evil enchantment.
    1. Gawain–Romances.   2. Arthurian romances.
[1. Gawain.   2. Arthur, King.   3. Folklore–England.
4. Knights and knighthood–Fiction]
I. Wijngaard, Juan, ill.   II. Title
PZ8.1.H268Si   1985   398.2′2   85-63
ISBN 0-688-07046-9

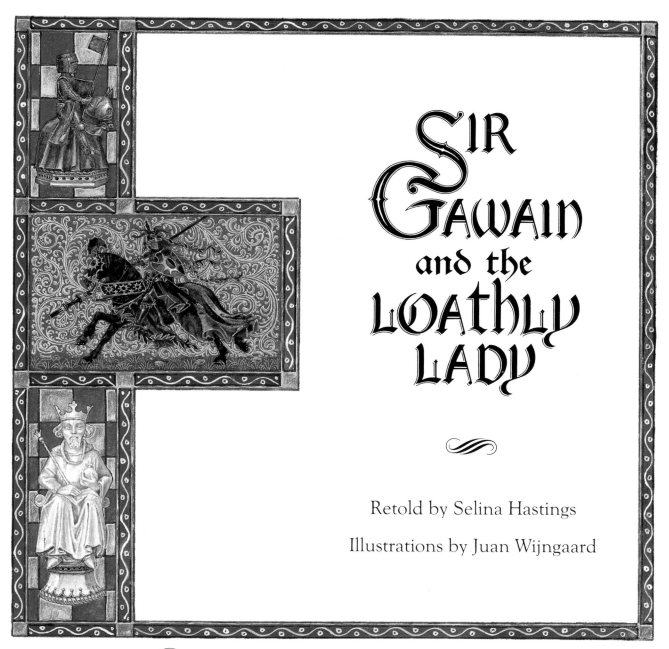

Sir Gawain and the Loathly Lady

Retold by Selina Hastings

Illustrations by Juan Wijngaard

A Mulberry Paperback Book · New York

KING ARTHUR and his court had moved to the castle of Carlisle for Christmas. Every evening there was feasting and dancing, while by day the King and his knights rode out into the Inglewood to hunt. One morning the King, galloping fast in pursuit of a young stag, found himself separated from his companions, his quarry having outrun the hounds and disappeared. Reining in his horse, he saw that he was in an unfamiliar part of the forest, on the edge of a black and brackish pond surrounded by pine trees whose dark foliage obscured the light of day. Suddenly Arthur noticed in the shadows on the other side of the pond a man on horseback, watching him. The man was covered from head to foot in black armour, and he sat motionless on a charger which was itself as black as midnight.

All at once the stranger spurred forward, splashing through the muddy water towards the King. As he drew within hailing distance, he stopped.

7

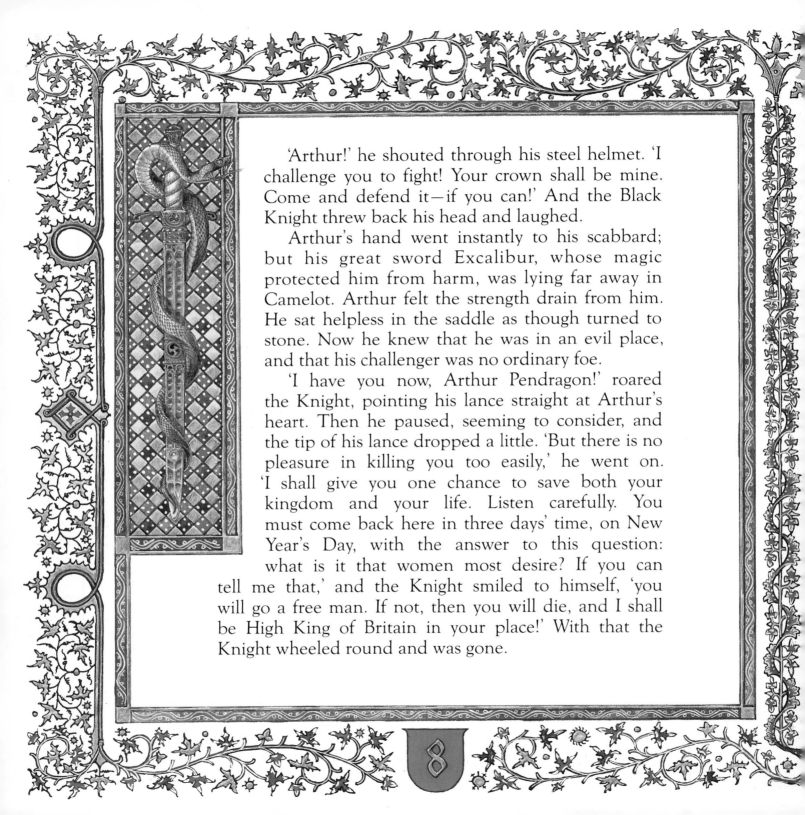

'Arthur!' he shouted through his steel helmet. 'I challenge you to fight! Your crown shall be mine. Come and defend it—if you can!' And the Black Knight threw back his head and laughed.

Arthur's hand went instantly to his scabbard; but his great sword Excalibur, whose magic protected him from harm, was lying far away in Camelot. Arthur felt the strength drain from him. He sat helpless in the saddle as though turned to stone. Now he knew that he was in an evil place, and that his challenger was no ordinary foe.

'I have you now, Arthur Pendragon!' roared the Knight, pointing his lance straight at Arthur's heart. Then he paused, seeming to consider, and the tip of his lance dropped a little. 'But there is no pleasure in killing you too easily,' he went on. 'I shall give you one chance to save both your kingdom and your life. Listen carefully. You must come back here in three days' time, on New Year's Day, with the answer to this question: what is it that women most desire? If you can tell me that,' and the Knight smiled to himself, 'you will go a free man. If not, then you will die, and I shall be High King of Britain in your place!' With that the Knight wheeled round and was gone.

Gradually Arthur felt his strength return. As he rode slowly homewards, he thought over the riddle whose solution would save his life. What *was* it that women most desired? On the way, he stopped every woman he met—a goose girl, an abbess on a grey mare, a merchant's fat wife with a retinue of servants—to ask what it was she most desired. And every one of them gave him a different answer.

When at last he reached the castle, to be greeted by Guinevere his Queen, he was careful to conceal the danger he was in, saying only that he had accepted a wager from an unknown knight to find within three days what it was that women most desired. The ladies of the court, pretty as peacocks in their brightly coloured silks and velvets, clustered round Arthur, eager to supply him with the answer. Some said beauty, some wealth, others wanted power or spiritual salvation. One lady, getting on in years, wished for a young husband. None could agree.

That night Arthur lay sleepless, his heart heavy at the thought of the terrible encounter in front of him. But true to his word he set off on New Year's morning to meet the Black Knight, knowing that still he had not heard the answer to the riddle, and that unless a miracle occurred his life would be lost.

Cantering along a grassy ride on the outskirts of the forest, he heard a woman's voice call his name, and looking round caught sight of a flash of red by the side of the road. Puzzled, Arthur drew up his horse and dismounted.

He walked back a few steps and saw in front of him, sitting on a tree stump, a woman in a scarlet dress. She looked up at him — and Arthur gasped.

She was the ugliest living thing he had ever set eyes on, a freak, a monster, a truly loathly lady.

12

Her nose was like a pig's snout; from a misshapen mouth stuck out two yellowing rows of horse's teeth; her cheeks were covered in sores; she had only one eye, rheumy and red-rimmed, and from a naked scalp hung a few lank strands of hair. Her whole body was swollen and bent out of shape, and her fingers, on which were several fine rings, were as gnarled and twisted as the roots of an old oak.

'My lord King,' said the hag in a surprisingly sweet voice, 'why do you look so dismayed?'

Quickly Arthur explained that he had been deep in thought, and he told the Loathly Lady about his quest, how he was honour-bound to accept the Black Knight's challenge, and how, without the answer to the question, he was sure to die. The Lady laughed.

'I can answer your question,' she said. 'There's no mystery to that! But if I do, you must promise to grant me one wish — whatever that wish may be.'

'Madam, you have my word,' the King eagerly replied. '*Anything* you ask shall be yours.'

The Lady whispered a few words in his ear. And then Arthur knew with absolute certainty that he had nothing more to fear. Joyfully he turned to go, but the Lady caught his sleeve.

13

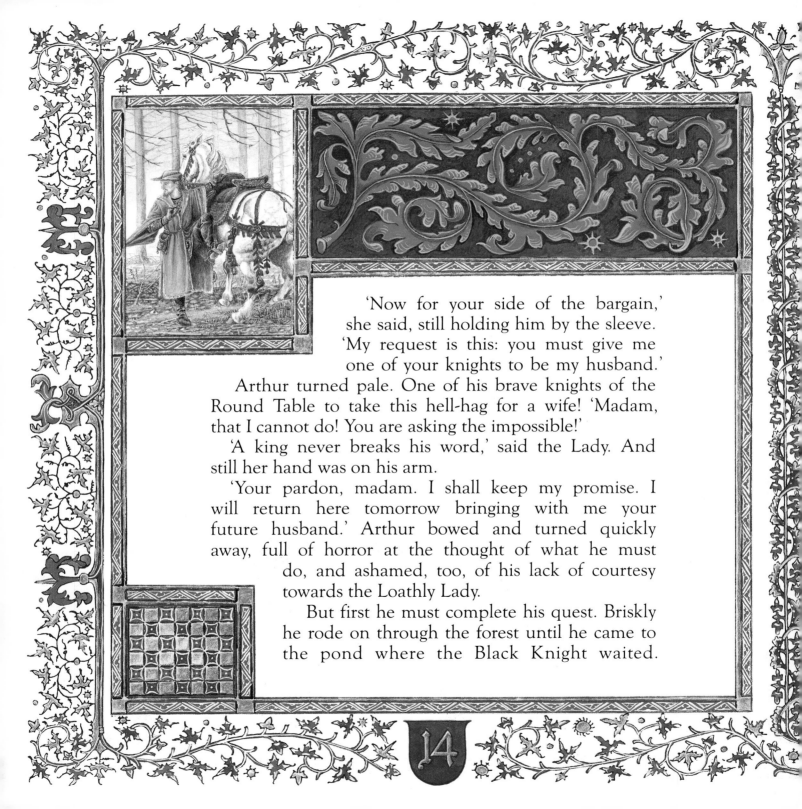

'Now for your side of the bargain,' she said, still holding him by the sleeve. 'My request is this: you must give me one of your knights to be my husband.'

Arthur turned pale. One of his brave knights of the Round Table to take this hell-hag for a wife! 'Madam, that I cannot do! You are asking the impossible!'

'A king never breaks his word,' said the Lady. And still her hand was on his arm.

'Your pardon, madam. I shall keep my promise. I will return here tomorrow bringing with me your future husband.' Arthur bowed and turned quickly away, full of horror at the thought of what he must do, and ashamed, too, of his lack of courtesy towards the Loathly Lady.

But first he must complete his quest. Briskly he rode on through the forest until he came to the pond where the Black Knight waited.

As before the Knight was sitting
on his great charger, deep in the
shadows of the trees. He watched Arthur
approach, his lance lifted in a mocking salute.

'Well, Arthur Pendragon, High King of Britain, have you come to surrender your kingdom?'

'I have the answer to your question,' Arthur quietly replied. For a moment there was silence: no bird song, no rustle of movement on the forest floor, not even the chink and creak of harness. 'What all women most desire is to have their own way.'

When he heard these words, the Black Knight let out a bellow of rage that rang throughout the Inglewood. 'God damn you, Arthur! May you roast in Hell! You have tricked me of my prize!' And with that he plunged off into the trees.

That evening Arthur sat before the fire in the great hall of the castle, gazing miserably into the flames. His life had been saved, but at a high cost. How could he condemn one of his knights to the embraces of the Loathly Lady? And yet he must keep his word. Guinevere, worried by her husband's melancholy air, knelt beside him, taking his hand in hers, and asked him the cause of his distress.

'My honour is at stake,' he said. 'I do not know how I may save it.'

Sir Gawain, the youngest of the company, was sitting close by playing chess. On hearing Arthur's words he leapt up, scattering the ivory chessmen at his feet. 'Sire, I beg you, let *me* defend you! Grant *me* the quest, that I may be the one to save the honour of my King!'

17

Arthur loved this knight, always the first to come forward, ever ready to put his courage to the test; and his heart sank. He saw Gawain's youth, his face so full of innocence and hope, and he remembered the frightful features of the Lady in the forest. But Arthur had no choice. Taking a deep breath he began the tale of his meeting with the Black Knight, of the challenge, and of how the Loathly Lady came to his rescue, of her terrible deformity, and the price she demanded for saving his life. As he talked, the other knights and their ladies drew near to listen. When he had finished, not a word was spoken. Those who were married looked thankfully at their wives; those who were not prayed that the young man's courage would not desert him.

Gawain looked stunned, but his spirit never faltered. 'Take me to her, Sire,' he said. 'I will marry her tomorrow.'

18

The next morning Arthur and Gawain, with Sir Kay, the King's steward, and a small company of knights escorting a richly decorated litter, set out for the Forest of Inglewood. The day was crisp and bright and the sun shone in a cloudless sky, but the little band was melancholy. All too soon Arthur caught sight of the flash of scarlet, and there she was, the Loathly Lady, sitting on her tree stump by the side of the road. Arthur dismounted and kissed the gnarled hand she held out. Behind him the knights sat still as statues, hardly able to believe their eyes.

'Good God, Sire!' burst out Sir Kay, never famous for the kindness of his tongue. 'The woman's a monster! We can't bring *her* to live among the ladies of our court!'

19

Before Arthur could rebuke his steward, Gawain jumped down from his horse and knelt before the Lady. 'Madam,' he said, 'will you honour me with your hand in marriage?'

20

'Oh, Sir Gawain, not you. Have you, too, come to mock me?' said the Lady. But when she looked into the knight's honest face, she knew he had spoken sincerely, so she gave him her hand and let him lead her to the litter which was waiting to carry her to the castle.

As the little party rode through the narrow streets of the town, the Lady hid her face in her hands so none could see her ugliness. But when they reached the castle yard, she was obliged to step into view, and trembled as she heard the gasps of horror that greeted her appearance. Only Guinevere appeared to notice nothing: she gave no shiver of disgust as she welcomed the poor monster and took her hand to lead her to the bridal chamber. For Gawain and the Lady were to be married that night.

The wedding of Sir Gawain and the Loathly Lady was a dismal occasion. Gawain moved as though in a trance, and not all the jewels nor the fine velvet robe given her by the Queen could disguise the hideousness of the bride as she stumbled through the great hall on the arm of her husband. After the ceremony there was a feast; but no one had the appetite to eat. And after the feast the musicians began to play; but no one had the heart to dance.

Then Gawain seemed to shake himself awake, and gently leading his wife into the centre of the hall, he guided her through the slow steps of a courtly measure. Arthur followed with Guinevere, and then all the knights with their ladies, so that the grotesque sight of the limping, lurching Loathly Lady should not remain thus pitifully exposed.

de guſtibus non diſputandum

23

As midnight struck, and the hour could no longer be postponed, the King and Queen dismissed the company, and then escorted the couple to their chamber. Arthur gloomily embraced Gawain and wished him a good night, while Guinevere kissed the bride on both her pitted cheeks — and then they left them, alone together.

The chamber had been decorated with fresh leaves; sweet-smelling rushes were strewn on the floor; the great carved bed, hung with velvet, was covered in soft furs. But Gawain saw none of this. With a groan he flung himself into a chair in front of the fire. What was he to do? What did the code of chivalry demand? Was he to spend the rest of his life shackled to a creature more hideous than the demon of a nightmare? Just then he heard a rustle of silk behind him, and his wife's sweet voice: 'Will you not come to bed, my lord?'

24

Shuddering with horror he slowly turned his head. Standing before him was the most beautiful woman he had ever seen. She had long golden hair hanging to her waist, her figure was slender as a fairy's, her pale skin as perfect as a piece of polished ivory.

25

Slowly placing her arms about his neck, she kissed him gently on the cheek. 'I am your wife, Sir Gawain. This is the Loathly Lady whom you see before you. By marrying me you have half-released me from a spell which doomed me to that disgusting shape in which King Arthur found me. But only half-released.' She looked down and sadly sighed. 'I must return to that foul form for half of every day unless you can answer me one question.'

'My wife,' whispered Gawain wonderingly, gazing at the Lady's lovely face. 'My dearest wife, what is your question?'

'You must tell me this: would you rather have me beautiful by day and hideous by night? Or would you have me beautiful at night, as I am now, and my old ugly shape during the day?' The Lady took a step back, and regarded Gawain intently.

'Oh, my love, how can I tell?' said Gawain, distracted by the choice before him. Then, recalling that it was his wedding night, and drawing near to take her in his arms, he said, 'Come to me at night beautiful as you are now.'

The Lady frowned, and took another step back. 'That is strangely uncharitable of you, sir. Do you condemn me to the contempt of the whole court, to be mocked and despised everywhere I go, unable to let darkness hide

my shame? That is not what I expect a loving husband to wish for me, that I should suffer in this way!'

'Oh, forgive me,' cried Gawain, penitent. 'That was cruelly thoughtless of me. Be beautiful by day, my love, and at night resume your old shape.' He held out a hand to her.

But still the Lady was not pleased; she did not take his hand. 'Oh, husband,' said she, 'do you love your wife so little that you care not how vile she looks lying beside you? Are you so indifferent as to be content with an ugly witch as the companion of your private hours? Do you not consider *my* feelings at having to come to you every night repellent and deformed?'

Gawain, at a loss for words, hung his head. Whichever choice he made — by day, by night — was wrong. 'Madam, I am unable to answer your question. I must leave it to you. *You* must choose whichever you prefer.'

At this the Lady laughed and clapped her hands with joy. 'That,' she cried, flinging her arms about his neck, 'is the right answer to my question. You have given me what every woman wants — her own way. And now the spell is broken. You will never see that hideous old hag again. I am my true self — and will be yours for ever.'

The next morning Arthur, anxious to know how Gawain had survived the night, wondered that such a reluctant bridegroom should stay in his chamber so late, expecting rather that he would leave the side of his Loathly Lady as soon as courtesy allowed. But when at midday Gawain finally appeared, leading his bride into the hall, Arthur wondered no more. The pair were so happy and so much in love. Now he saw that all was well—his kingdom safe, the Lady free of her enchantment, and ahead of them a night of celebration such as the castle of Carlisle had never known before.

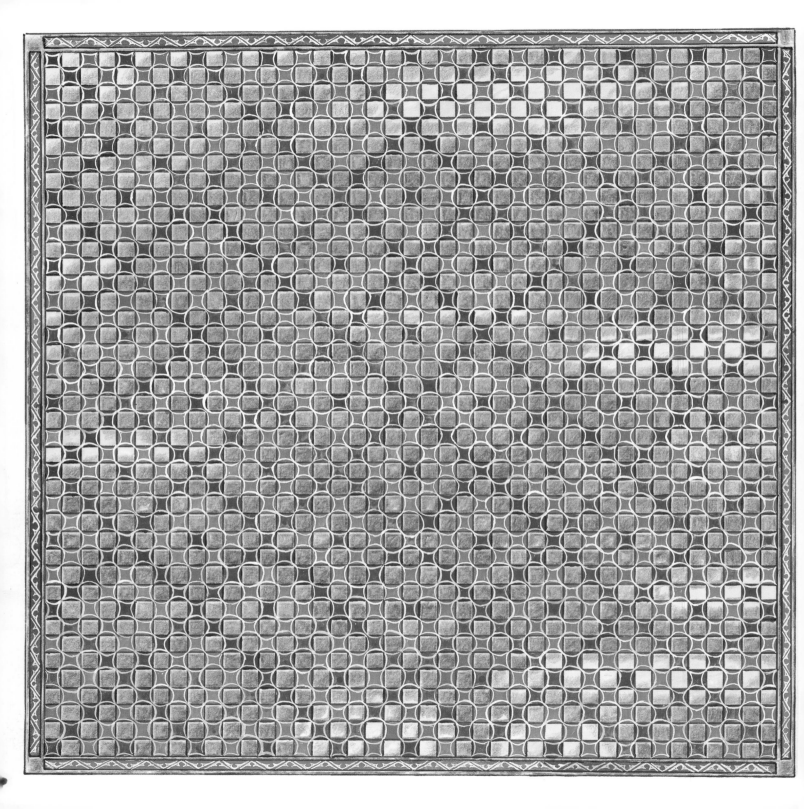

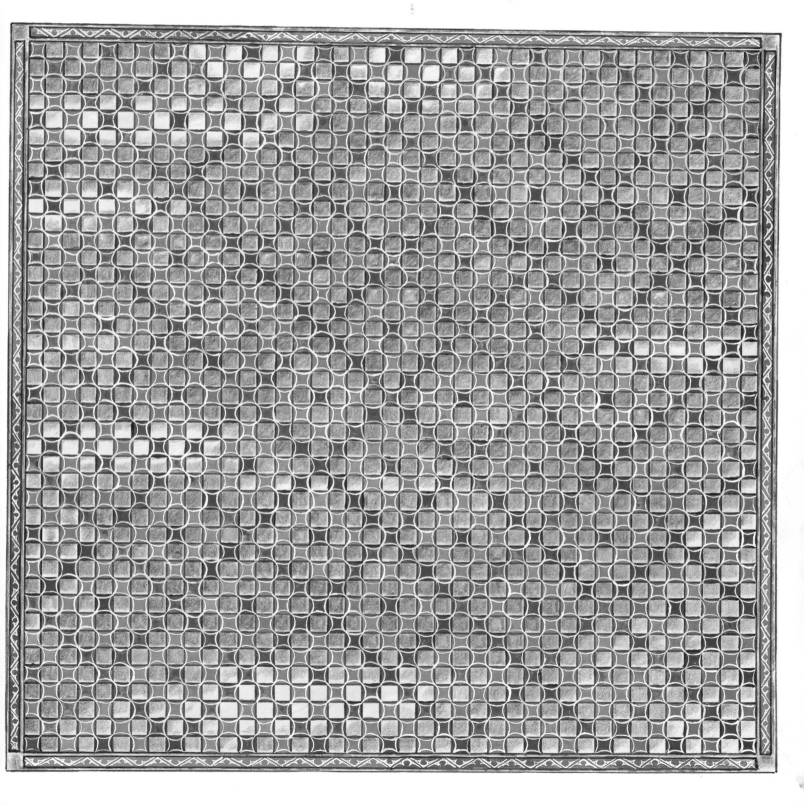